Y0-DWW-761

Bryce HARPER

by Matt Scheff

SportsZone
An Imprint of Abdo Publishing
abdopublishing.com

abdopublishing.com

Published by Abdo Publishing, a division of ABDO, PO Box 398166, Minneapolis, Minnesota 55439. Copyright © 2016 by Abdo Consulting Group, Inc. International copyrights reserved in all countries. No part of this book may be reproduced in any form without written permission from the publisher. SportsZone™ is a trademark and logo of Abdo Publishing.

Printed in the United States of America, North Mankato, Minnesota
082015
012016

**THIS BOOK CONTAINS
RECYCLED MATERIALS**

Cover Photos: Gregory Bull/AP Images, background; Andrew A. Nelles/AP Images, foreground
Interior Photos: Gregory Bull/AP Images, 1 (background); Andrew A. Nelles/AP Images, 1 (foreground); Alex Brandon/
AP Images, 4-5, 6-7, 22, 23; Josh Holmberg/Icon Sportswire, 8-9; Seth Poppel/Yearbook Library, 10; Josh Holmberg/
Icon SMI/Newscom, 11; Isaac Brekken/AP Images, 12, 13; Matt York/AP Images, 14-15; Mike Janes/Four Seam Images/AP
Images, 16-17; Louis Lopez/Cal Sport Media/AP Images, 18-19, 20-21; Frank Franklin II/AP Images, 24-25; Nick Wass/AP
Images, 26-27, 28-29

Editor: Patrick Donnelly
Series Designer: Laura Polzin

Library of Congress Control Number: 2015945985

Cataloging-in-Publication Data
Scheff, Matt.
 Bryce Harper / Matt Scheff.
  p. cm. -- (Baseball's greatest stars)
Includes index.
ISBN 978-1-68078-075-8
1. Harper, Bryce, 1992- --Juvenile literature. 2. Baseball players--United States--Biography--Juvenile literature.   I.
Title.
796.357092--dc23
[B]   2015945985

CONTENTS

STARTING WITH A BANG 4

EARLY LIFE 8

TOP PROSPECT 14

ROOKIE SENSATION 20

BIG-LEAGUE SUPERSTAR 24

Timeline 30
Glossary 31
Index 32
About the Author 32

STARTING WITH A BANG

Washington Nationals fans packed the stadium for Opening Day in 2013. They had not seen many winners since the Nationals had moved to Washington in 2005. But now the future was bright. The team was loaded with young stars. The most promising was 20-year-old Bryce Harper.

The crowd roared as Harper stepped to the plate in the first inning. Miami Marlins pitcher Ricky Nolasco delivered a pitch. CRACK! Harper crushed it. The ball sailed 385 feet and cleared the right-field scoreboard. It was a home run!

Harper is congratulated by teammate Ryan Zimmerman after his first Opening Day home run in 2013.

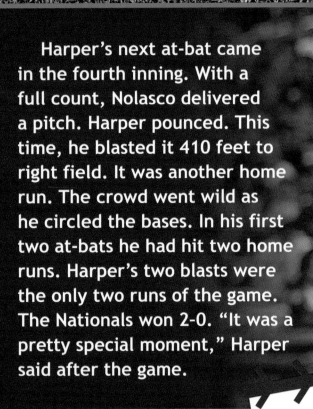

Harper's next at-bat came in the fourth inning. With a full count, Nolasco delivered a pitch. Harper pounced. This time, he blasted it 410 feet to right field. It was another home run. The crowd went wild as he circled the bases. In his first two at-bats he had hit two home runs. Harper's two blasts were the only two runs of the game. The Nationals won 2-0. "It was a pretty special moment," Harper said after the game.

FAST FACT

Harper's favorite movie is *The Sandlot*. It tells the story of a group of kids who play baseball together.

Harper hits his second home run of the game against the Marlins on Opening Day in 2013.

EARLY LIFE

Bryce Aron Max Harper was born on October 16, 1992, in Las Vegas, Nevada. He started playing tee ball when he was just three years old. Bryce often played on teams with his brother Bryan, who is three years older. The age difference hardly mattered. Bryce was always one of the best players on the field.

FAST FACT

Bryce's father, Ron, was a Las Vegas ironworker. Bryce credits his dad with teaching him a strong work ethic.

Bryce rounds the bases after hitting a home run for Las Vegas High School.

Bryce attended Las Vegas High School. He was a great all-around athlete. His best sport was baseball. He played outfield and catcher. His amazing raw power wowed fans, opponents, and big-league scouts. He was just a 16-year-old sophomore when he appeared on the cover of the national magazine *Sports Illustrated*. The headline read "Baseball's Chosen One."

Bryce represented Team USA in international competitions while he was still in high school.

FAST FACT

As a freshman in high school, Bryce smashed a 570-foot home run!

Bryce played catcher at Las Vegas High School.

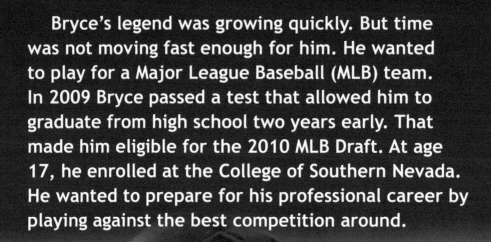

Bryce's legend was growing quickly. But time was not moving fast enough for him. He wanted to play for a Major League Baseball (MLB) team. In 2009 Bryce passed a test that allowed him to graduate from high school two years early. That made him eligible for the 2010 MLB Draft. At age 17, he enrolled at the College of Southern Nevada. He wanted to prepare for his professional career by playing against the best competition around.

Bryce shows off his strong arm in a game at the College of Southern Nevada.

Bryce continued to pound opposing pitchers in his one college season.

FAST FACT

Bryce made the most of his year in college. In 66 games, he belted 31 home runs. In one playoff game, he went 6-for-6 with four home runs, a double, and a triple!

TOP PROSPECT

Some scouts thought Harper was the best power prospect they'd seen in years. The Nationals chose him with the first pick in the 2010 MLB Draft. Harper had played mostly catcher in college. But the Nationals wanted him to be a full-time outfielder. Harper worked on his outfield skills in the Arizona Fall League that year. Teams send many of their best young players there to gain more experience.

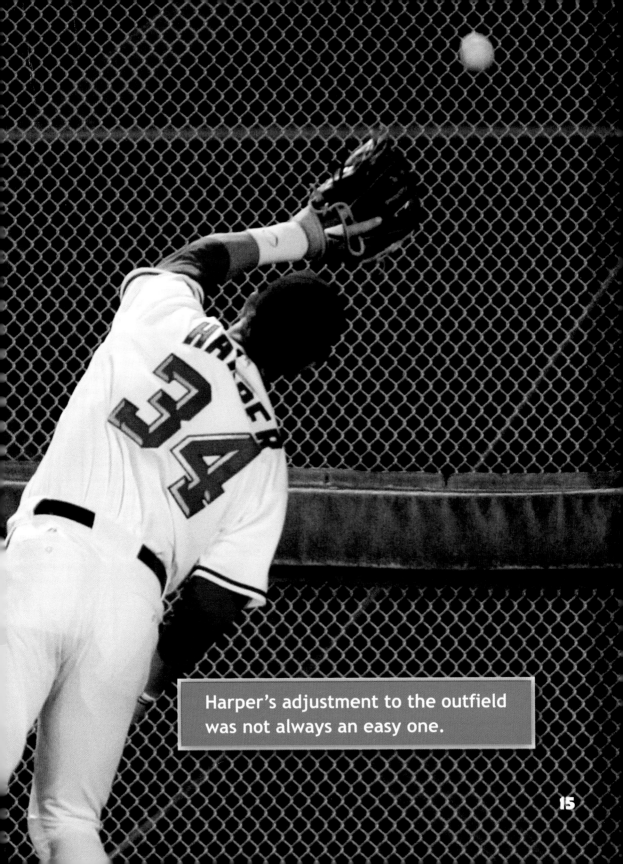

Harper's adjustment to the outfield was not always an easy one.

Harper started off slowly in the minor leagues in 2011. He had trouble seeing the ball. An eye doctor gave him contact lenses. It made a huge difference. During the next 20 games, Harper batted .480 with seven home runs. The rising star earned a spot in the 2011 MLB All-Star Futures Game.

A hamstring injury limited Harper to just 109 games in the minor leagues that year. But he still had a good year. Harper batted .297 with 17 home runs. And his extra work in the outfield paid off. He played mostly in left field and right field.

Harper gets a lead off third base for the Harrisburg Senators in 2011.

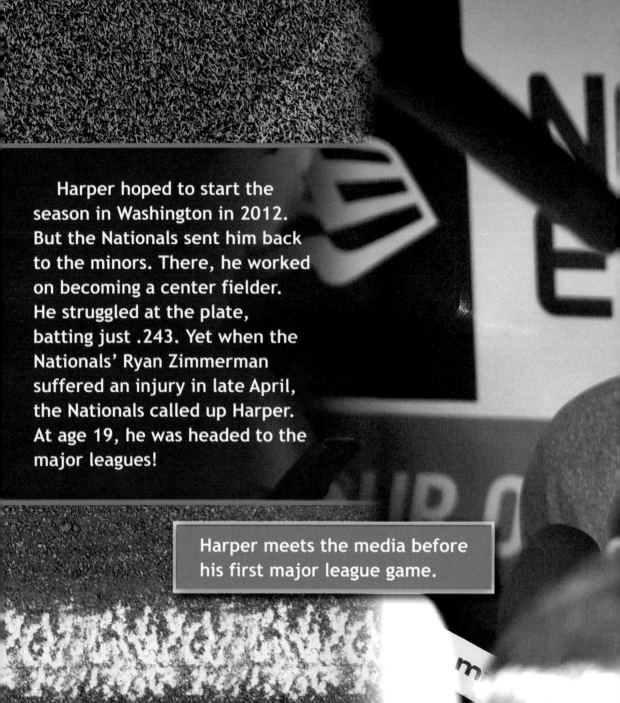

Harper hoped to start the season in Washington in 2012. But the Nationals sent him back to the minors. There, he worked on becoming a center fielder. He struggled at the plate, batting just .243. Yet when the Nationals' Ryan Zimmerman suffered an injury in late April, the Nationals called up Harper. At age 19, he was headed to the major leagues!

Harper meets the media before his first major league game.

ROOKIE SENSATION

Harper made his debut on April 28 in Los Angeles against the Dodgers. In his third at-bat, he ripped a double for his first big-league hit. Later, he drove in his first run. Nationals fans were excited.

But not everyone was thrilled to see the youngster succeed. Some people thought Harper was too confident and did not respect his opponents. In May, Philadelphia Phillies pitcher Cole Hamels hit Harper with a pitch on purpose. Harper made Hamels pay. He stole home plate later in the inning. He became the first teenager to steal home in 48 years.

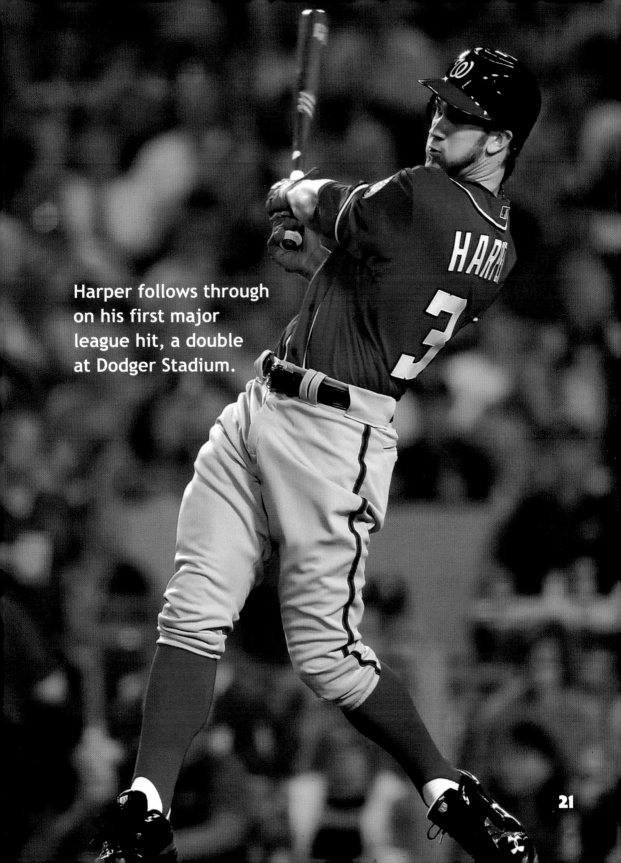

Harper follows through on his first major league hit, a double at Dodger Stadium.

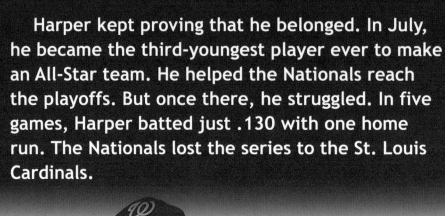

Harper kept proving that he belonged. In July, he became the third-youngest player ever to make an All-Star team. He helped the Nationals reach the playoffs. But once there, he struggled. In five games, Harper batted just .130 with one home run. The Nationals lost the series to the St. Louis Cardinals.

Harper shows off his All-Star jersey during his rookie season.

FAST FACT
Harper was named the 2012 National League (NL) Rookie of the Year.

Harper receives his 2012 NL Rookie of the Year Award on Opening Day in 2013.

BIG-LEAGUE SUPERSTAR

Harper was voted an All-Star starter in 2013. He also competed in the Home Run Derby. Harper thrilled fans with 16 home runs in the opening rounds. But he lost to Oakland's Yoenis Cespedes in the finals, 9-8. Knee and hip injuries slowed down Harper for much of the season. In 118 games, he batted .274 and hit 20 home runs.

Harper put on a show during the Home Run Derby at the 2013 MLB All-Star Game.

In April 2014, Harper smacked a bases-loaded triple. But as he slid headfirst into third base, he jammed his thumb. He missed almost two months with the injury. Harper returned in late June. He helped power the Nationals to a division title and the playoffs. They faced the San Francisco Giants. Harper slugged three home runs in the series. But it was not enough. The Giants won the series and ended Washington's season.

FAST FACT

Harper's brother, Bryan, is a pitcher in the Nationals' minor league system.

Harper injured his left thumb on this slide in a game against the San Diego Padres in April 2014.

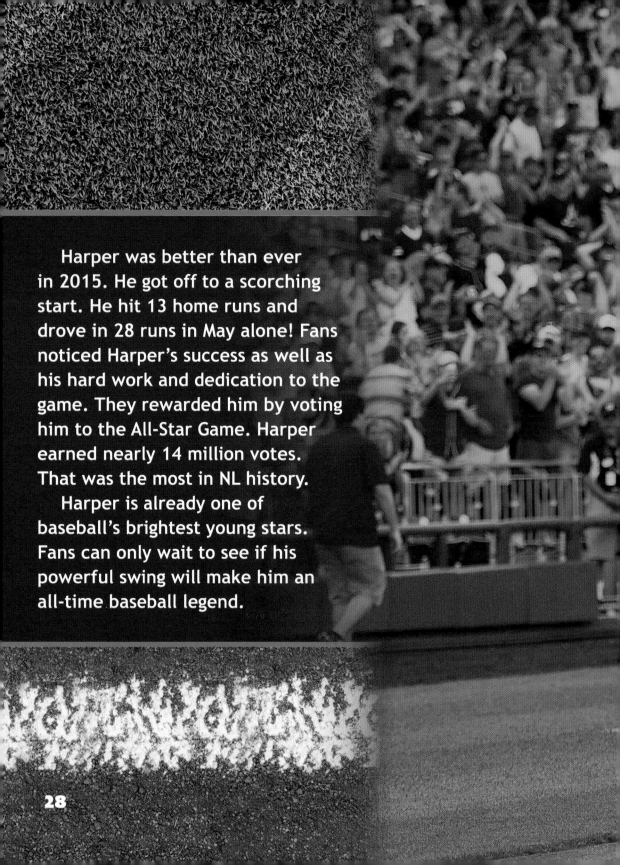

Harper was better than ever in 2015. He got off to a scorching start. He hit 13 home runs and drove in 28 runs in May alone! Fans noticed Harper's success as well as his hard work and dedication to the game. They rewarded him by voting him to the All-Star Game. Harper earned nearly 14 million votes. That was the most in NL history.

Harper is already one of baseball's brightest young stars. Fans can only wait to see if his powerful swing will make him an all-time baseball legend.

The crowd roars as Harper circles the bases after his walk-off home run beat the Atlanta Braves in May 2015.

TIMELINE

1992
Bryce Aron Max Harper is born on October 16, 1992, in Las Vegas, Nevada.

1996
Three-year-old Bryce starts playing tee ball with his older brother Bryan.

2009
At age 16, Bryce appears on the cover of *Sports Illustrated*. He earns his high school diploma after his sophomore year.

2010
Harper blasts 31 home runs for the College of Southern Nevada. The Nationals select him with the first pick in the 2010 MLB Draft.

2012
Harper makes his major league debut and goes on to win NL Rookie of the Year.

2013
Harper advances to the finals of the Home Run Derby but loses 9-8 to Yoenis Cespedes.

2014
Harper blasts three home runs in Washington's playoff series loss to the San Francisco Giants.

2015
Harper collects almost 14 million votes to the All-Star Game, the most in NL history.

GLOSSARY

DEBUT
First appearance.

DRAFT
The process by which leagues determine which teams will sign new players coming into the league.

FULL COUNT
A count of three balls and two strikes on a batter.

HAMSTRING
A tendon located at the back of the upper leg.

PROSPECT
A player regarded as likely to succeed in the future.

ROOKIE
A first-year player.

SCOUT
A person whose job is to evaluate talent.

INDEX

Arizona Fall League, 14
awards, 22

Cespedes, Yoenis, 24
College of Southern Nevada, 12

Hamels, Cole, 20
Harper, Bryan, 8, 26
Harper, Ron, 8

Las Vegas High School, 10
Las Vegas, Nevada, 8
Los Angeles Dodgers, 20

Miami Marlins, 4, 6
MLB Draft, 12, 14
MLB Home Run Derby, 24

NL All-Star team, 22, 24, 28
Nolasco, Ricky, 4, 6

Oakland Athletics, 24

Philadelphia Phillies, 20
playoffs, 22, 26

San Francisco Giants, 26
Sandlot, The, 6
Sports Illustrated, 10
St. Louis Cardinals, 22

Zimmerman, Ryan, 18

ABOUT THE AUTHOR

Matt Scheff is an artist and author living in Alaska. He enjoys mountain climbing, deep-sea fishing, and curling up with his two Siberian huskies to watch baseball.